EASY GUITAR
WITH NOTES & TAB

GREAT CLASSICAL THEMES

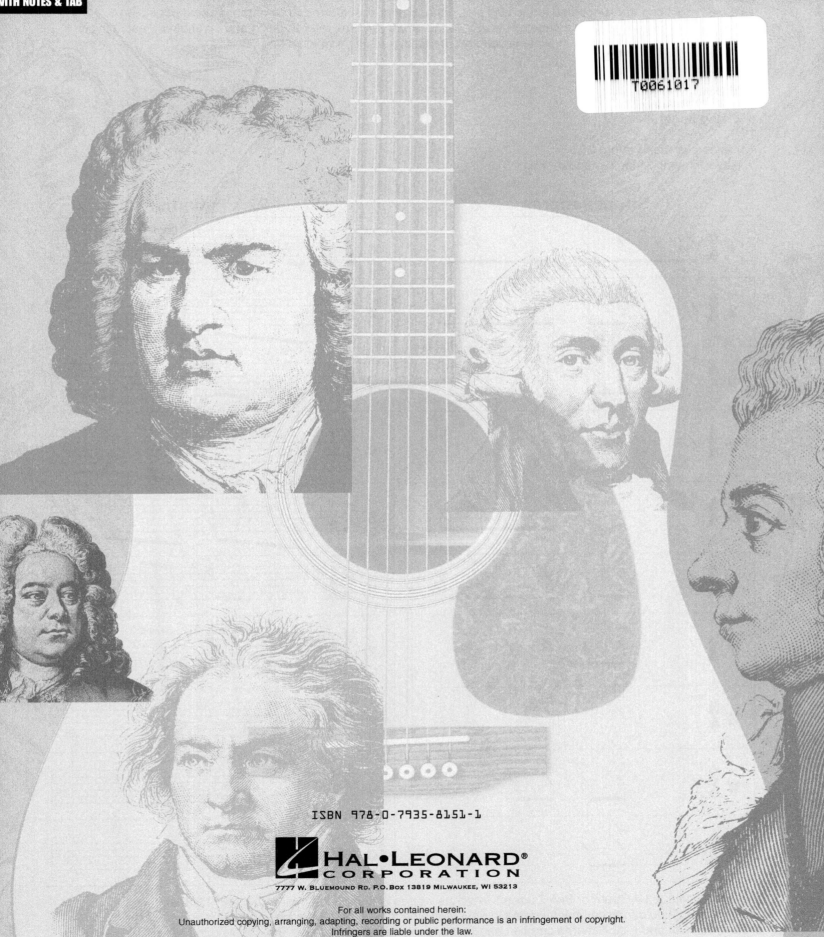

ISBN 978-0-7935-8151-1

HAL•LEONARD®
CORPORATION
7777 W. BLUEMOUND RD. P.O. BOX 13819 MILWAUKEE, WI 53213

Visit Hal Leonard Online at
www.halleonard.com

STRUM AND PICK PATTERNS

This chart contains the suggested strum and pick patterns that are referred to by number at the beginning of each song in this book. The symbols ⊓ and ∨ in the strum patterns refer to down and up strokes, respectively. The letters in the pick patterns indicate which right-hand fingers plays which strings.

p = thumb
i = index finger
m = middle finger
a = ring finger

For example; Pick Pattern 2
is played: thumb - index - middle - ring

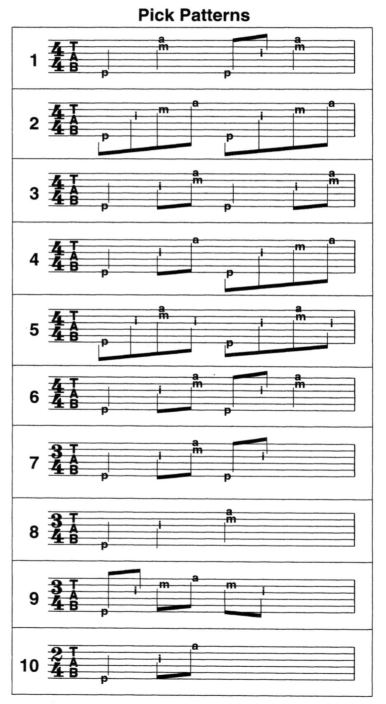

You can use the 3/4 Strum or Pick Patterns in songs written in compound meter (6/8, 9/8, 12/8, etc.).
For example, you can accompany a song in 6/8 by playing the 3/4 pattern twice in each measure.
The 4/4 Strum and Pick Patterns can be used for songs written in cut time (₵) by doubling the note time values in the patterns. Each pattern would therefore last two measures in cut time.

GREAT CLASSICAL THEMES

Ave Maria

By Franz Schubert

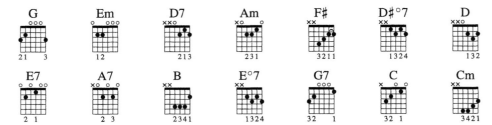

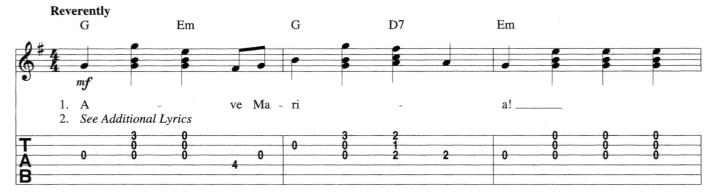

Strum Pattern: 1
Pick Pattern: 2

Verse
Reverently

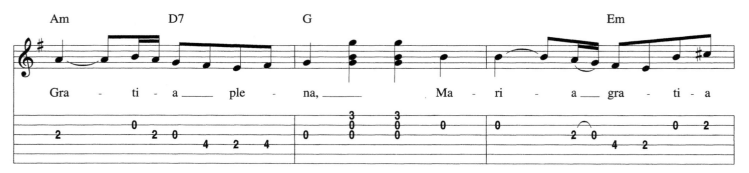

1. A - ve Ma - ri - a! _____
2. *See Additional Lyrics*

Gra - ti - a _____ ple - na, _____ Ma - ri - a gra - ti - a

ple - na, Ma - ri - a gra - ti - a _____ ple - na, _____ A -

ve, _____ A - ve! Do - mi - nus, _____ Do - mi - nus _____ te - cum, _____ Be - ne -

dic - ta tu in mu - li - e - re - bus et be - ne - dic -

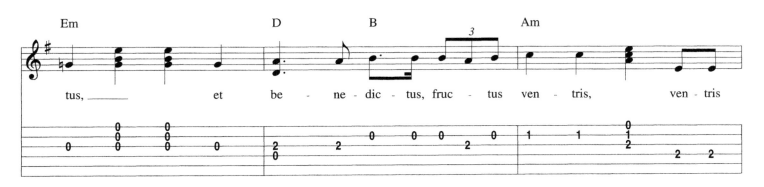

tus, _____ et be - ne - dic - tus, fruc - tus ven - tris, ven - tris

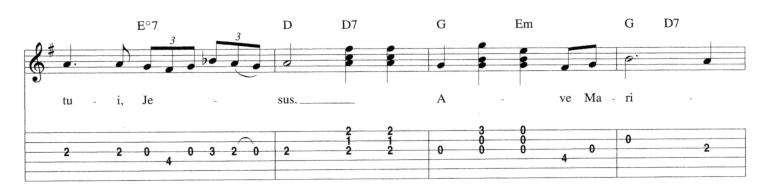

tu - i, Je - sus. _____ A - ve Ma - ri -

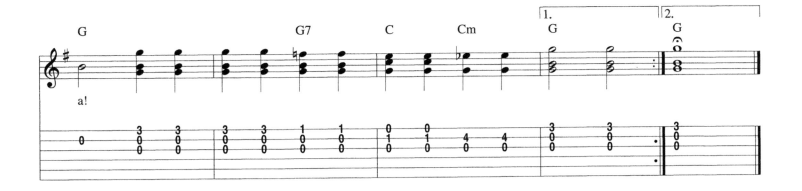

a!

Additional Lyrics

2. Ave Maria!
   Mater Dei, Ora pro nobis peccatoribus,
   Ora ora pro nobis, Ora, ra pro nobis peccatoribus.
   None et in hora mortis, in hora mortis nostrae,
   In hora mortis, mortis nostrae,
   In hora mortis nostrae.
   Ave Maria!

Bouree
(from Lute Suite No. 1)

Music by Johann Sebastian Bach

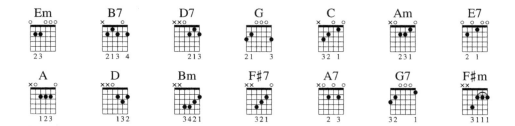

Strum Pattern: 3
Pick Pattern: 3

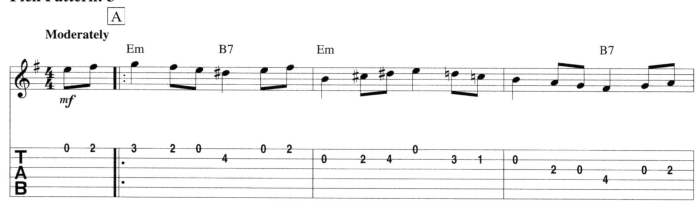

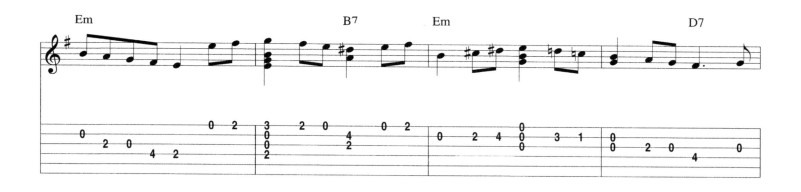

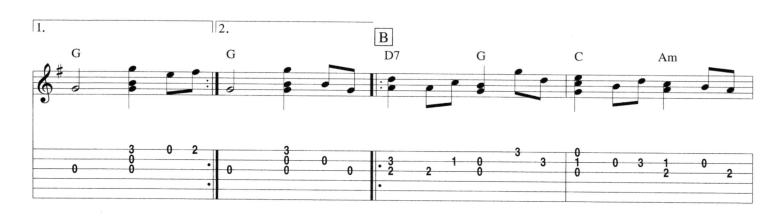

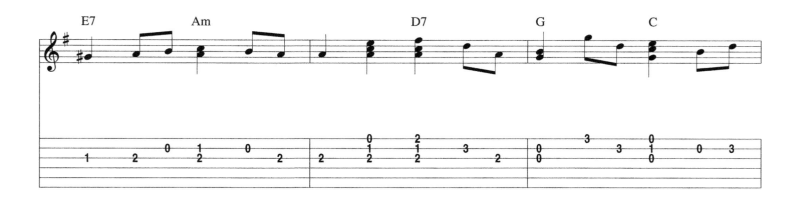

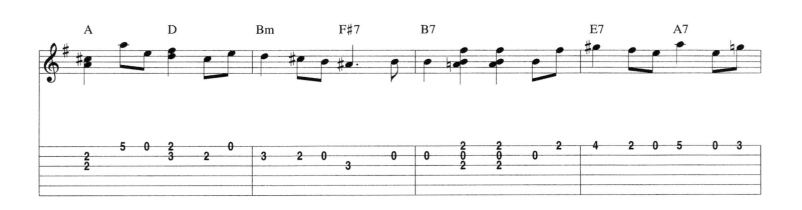

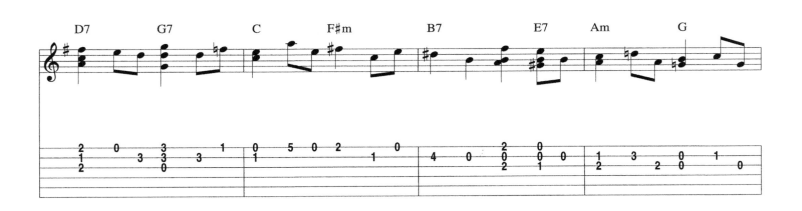

Canon in D

Music by Johann Pachelbel

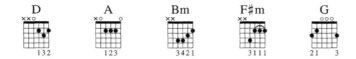

Strum Pattern: 1
Pick Pattern: 2

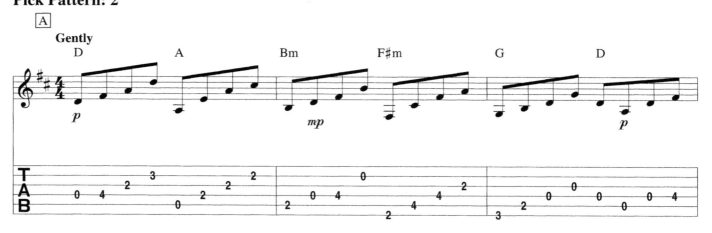

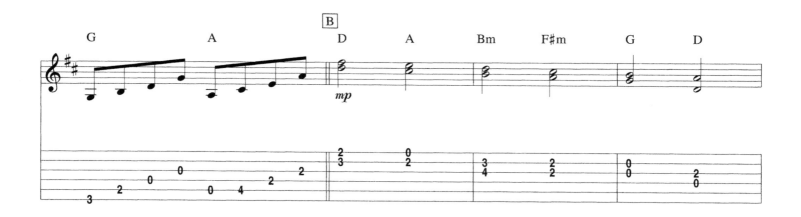

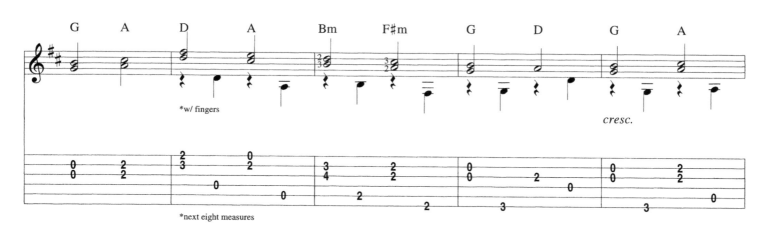

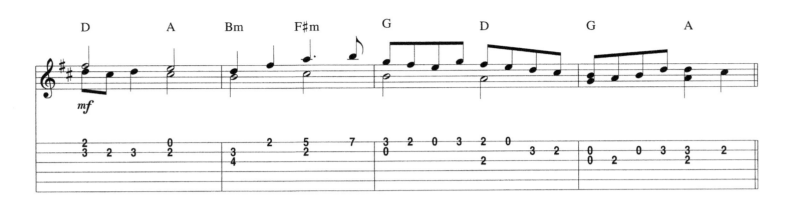

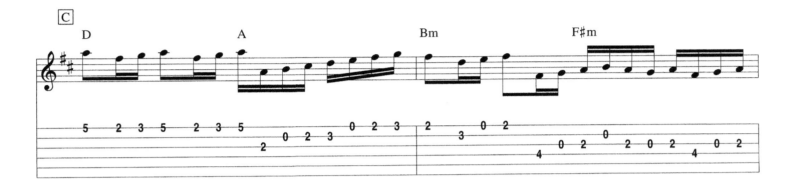

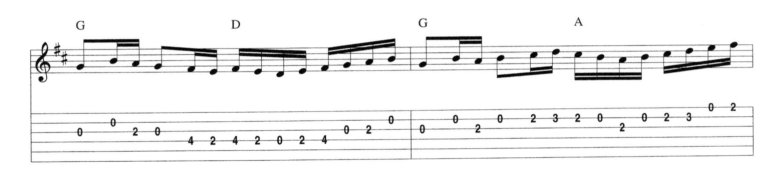

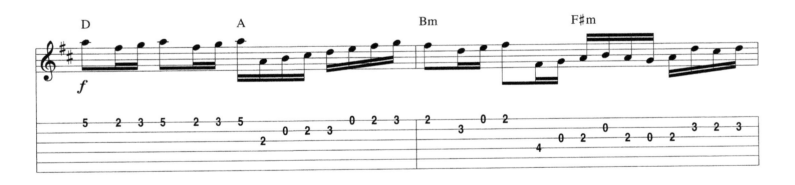

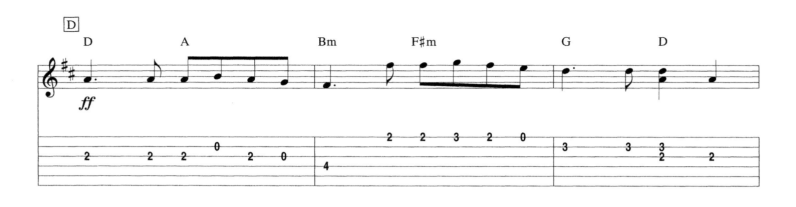

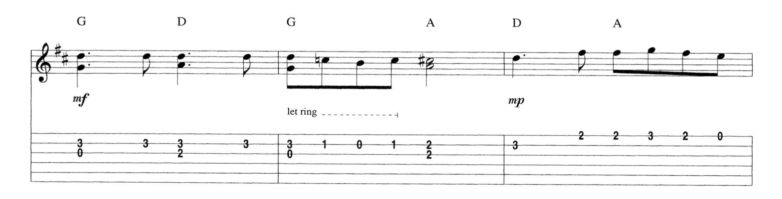

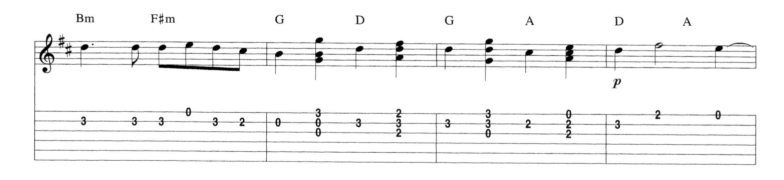

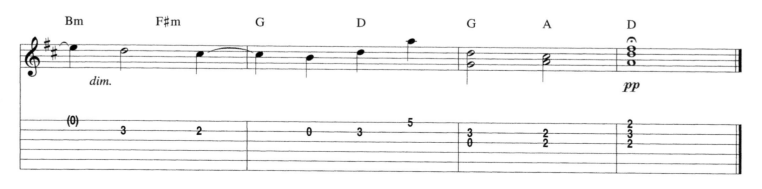

Concerto in D

(1st Movement)

Music by Antonio Vivaldi

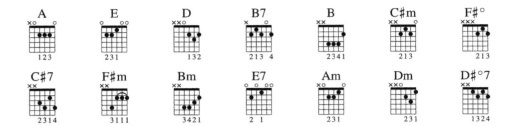

Strum Pattern: 3
Pick Pattern: 3

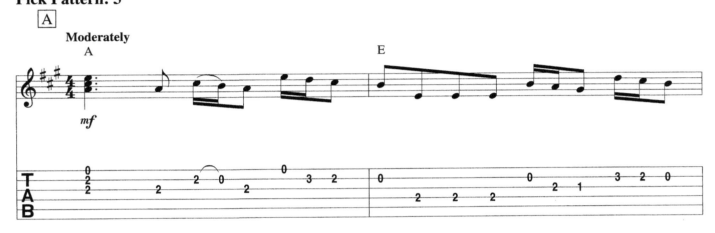

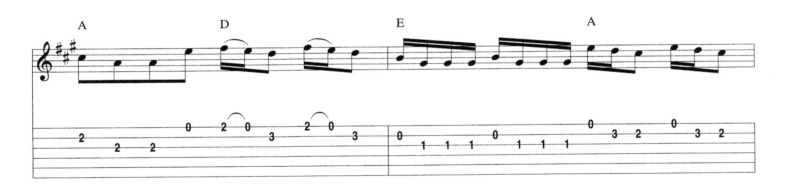

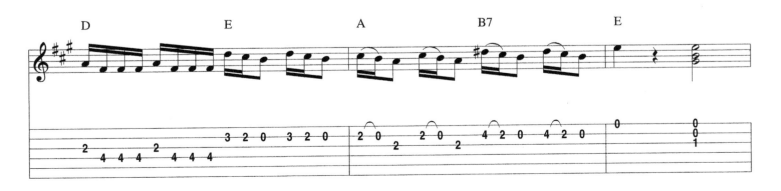

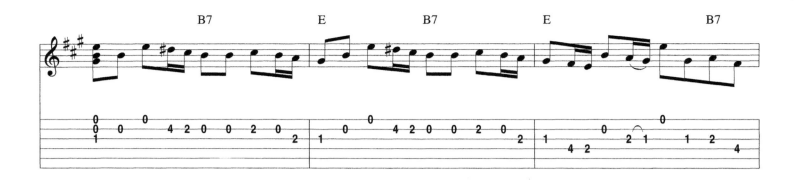

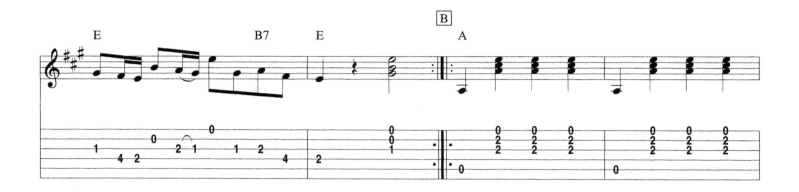

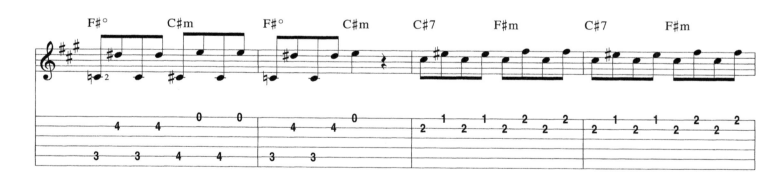

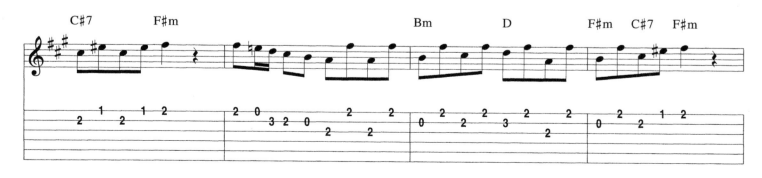

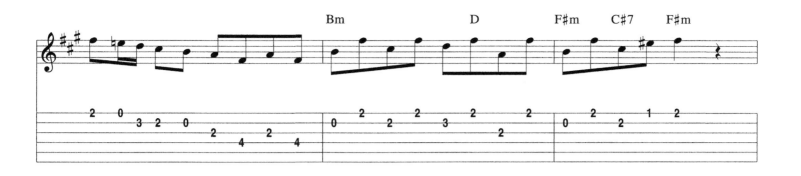

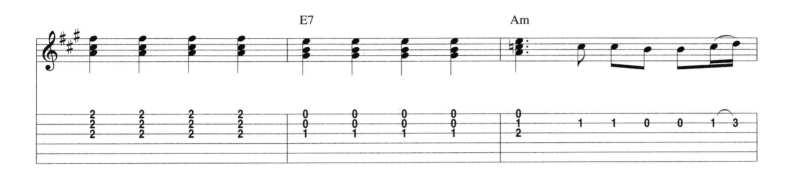

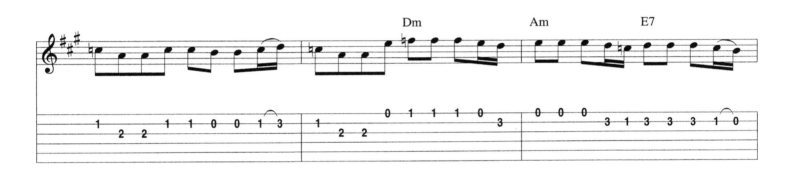

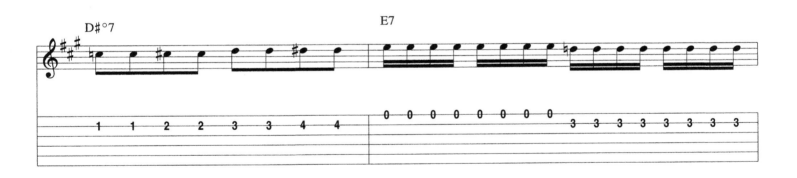

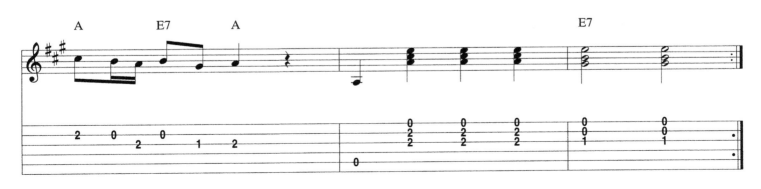

Clair de Lune

Music by Claude Debussy

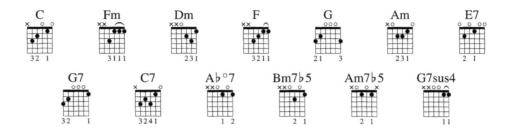

Strum Pattern: 7
Pick Pattern: 9

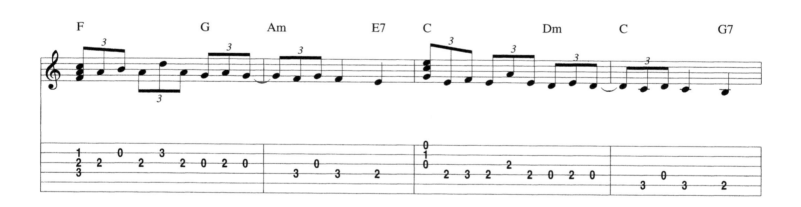

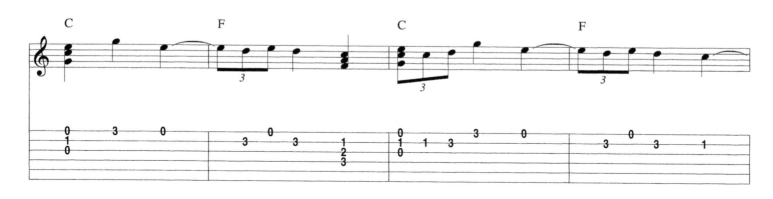

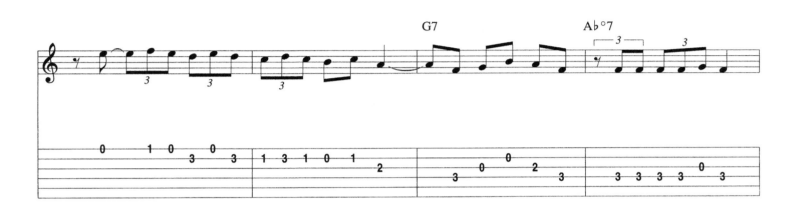

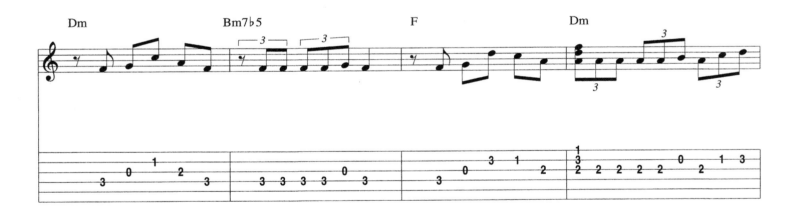

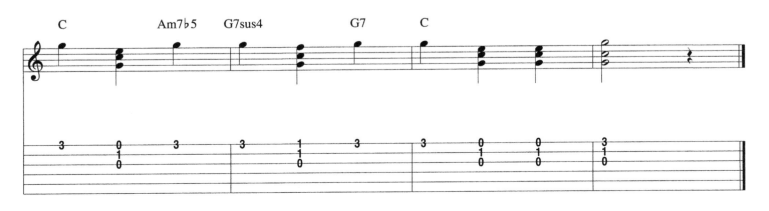

Concerto in D

(2nd Movement)

Music by Antonio Vivaldi

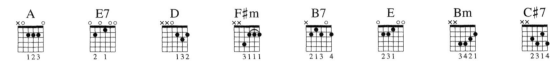

Strum Pattern: 3
Pick Pattern: 3

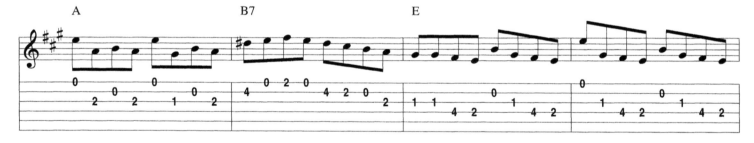

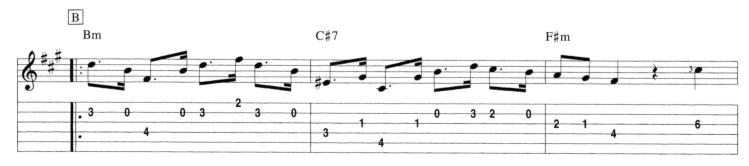

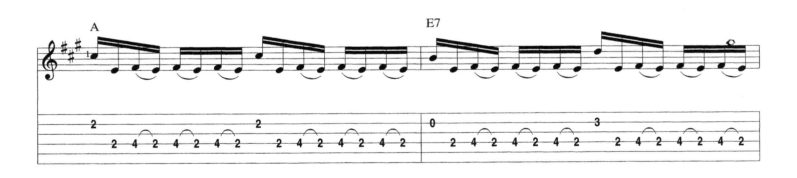

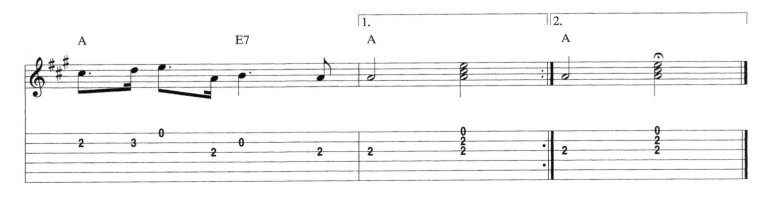

Eine Kleine Nachtmusik

Music by Wolfgang Amadeus Mozart

Strum Pattern: 4
Pick Pattern: 1

The Four Seasons

(Spring Theme)

Music by Antonio Vivaldi

Strum Pattern: 4
Pick Pattern: 1

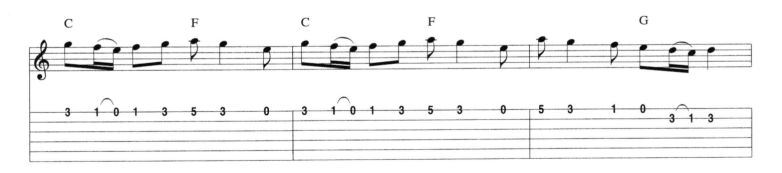

Für Elise

Music by Ludwig Van Beethoven

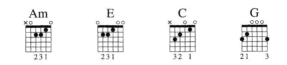

Strum Pattern: 7, 9
Pick Pattern: 7, 9

Moderately Slow

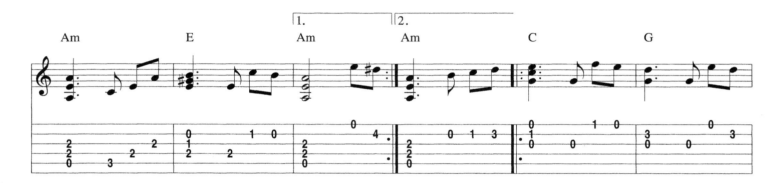

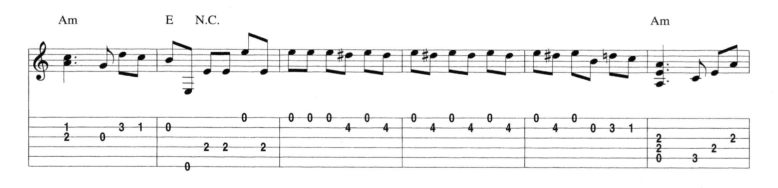

The Harmonious Blacksmith

Music by George Frideric Handel

Germany
(Einigkeit und Recht und Freiheit)

Music by Franz Joseph Haydn
Words by August Heinrich Hoffman von Fallersleben

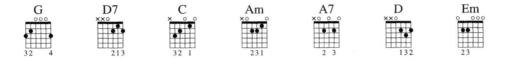

Strum Pattern: 4
Pick Pattern: 5

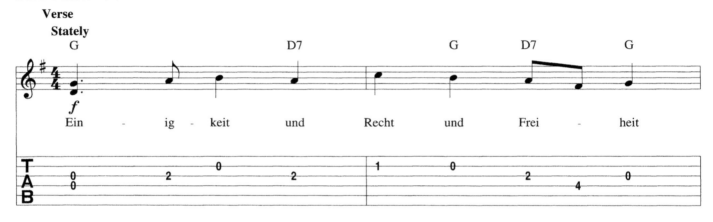

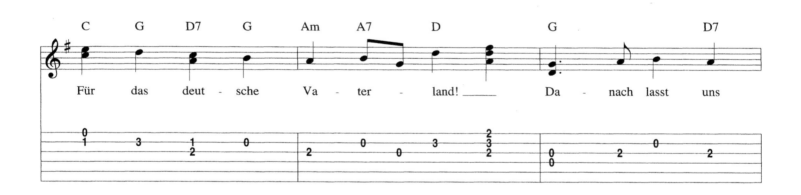

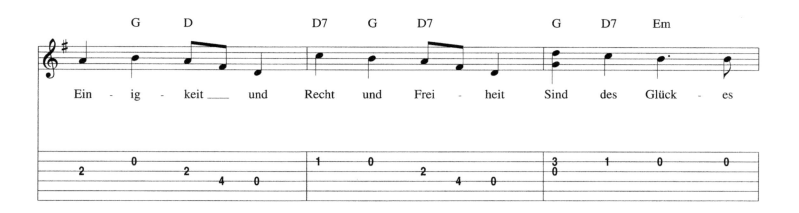

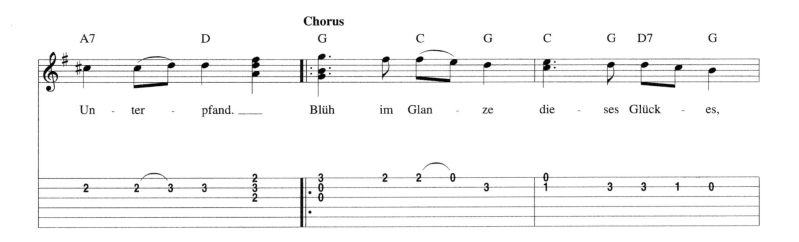

English Translation

Verse Unity and right and freedom
For the German Fatherland;
For this let us all fraternally strive
Each with heart and hand.
Unity and right and freedom
Are the pledge of happiness.

Chorus Bloom in the splendor of this happiness,
Germany, our Fatherland.

In the Hall of the Mountain King

(from Peer Gynt Suite)

Music by Edvard Grieg

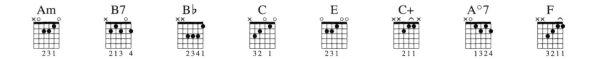

Strum Pattern: 3
Pick Pattern: 4

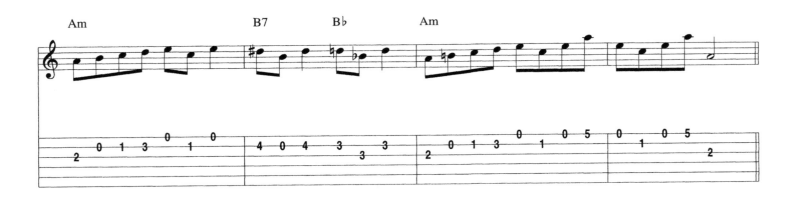

Jesu, Joy of Man's Desiring

By Johann Sebastian Bach

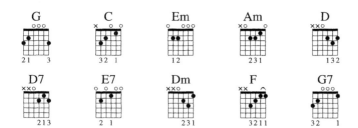

Strum Pattern: 8
Pick Pattern: 8

Intro
Moderately

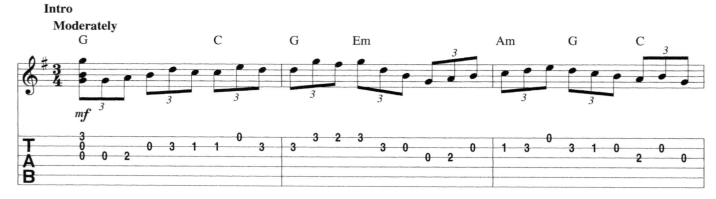

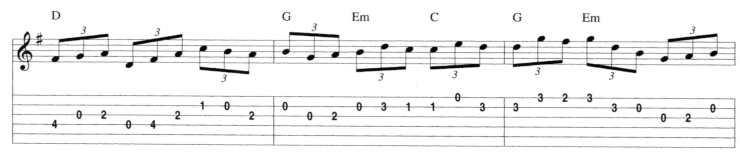

1. Je - su, joy of
2. *See Additional Lyrics*

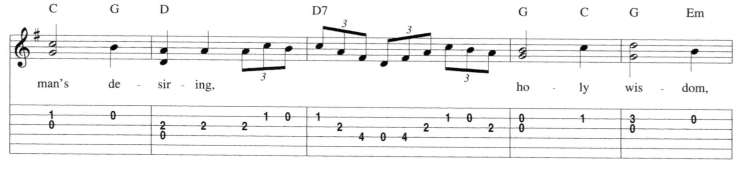

man's de - sir - ing,   ho - ly wis - dom,

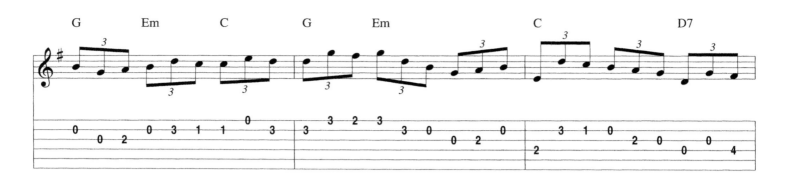

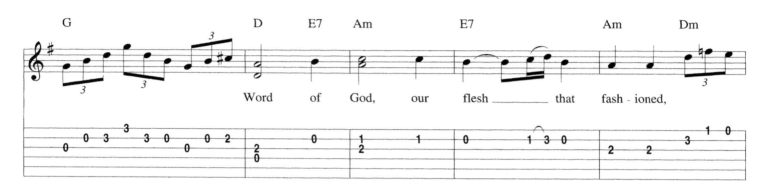

Word of God, our flesh _____ that fash - ioned,

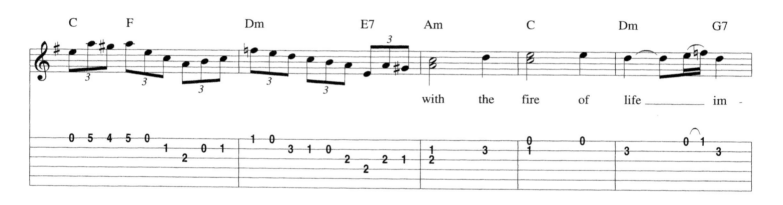

with the fire of life _____ im -

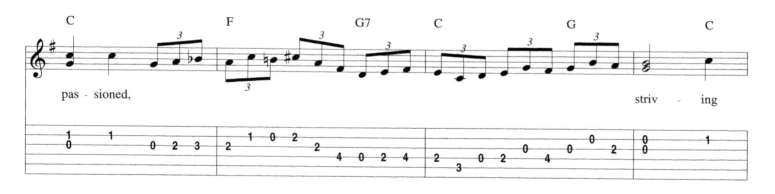

pas - sioned, striv - ing

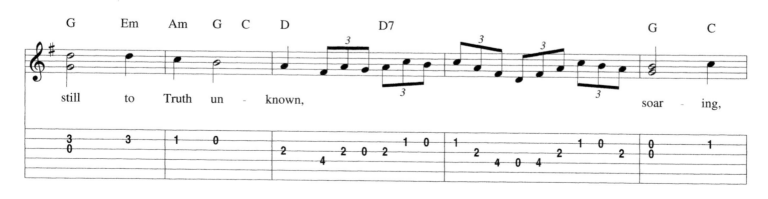

still to Truth un - known, soar - ing,

dy - ing round ___ Thy ___ throne.

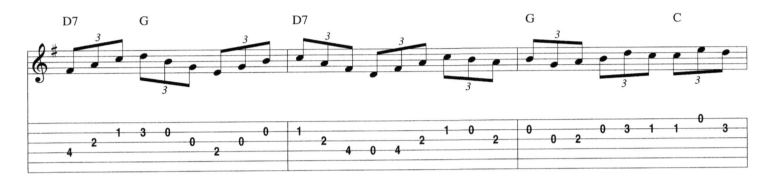

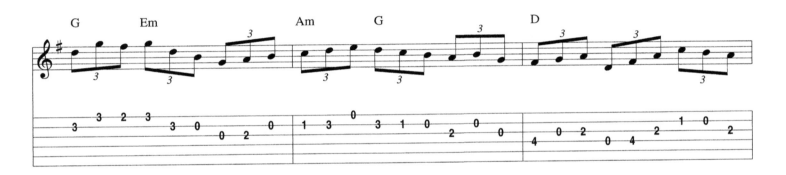

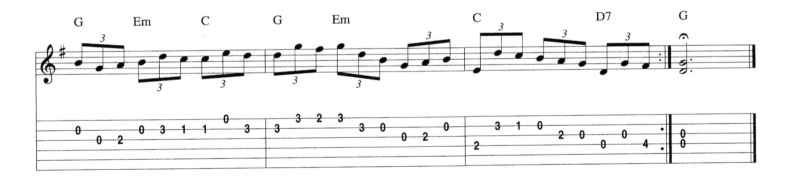

Additional Lyrics

2. Through the way where hope is guiding,
   Hark, what peaceful music rings!
   Where the flock in Thee confiding,
   Drink of joy from deathless springs.
   Their's is beauty's fairest pleasure,
   Their's is wisdom's holiest treasure.
   Thou dost ever lead Thine own,
   In the love of joys unknown.

Lullaby
(Wiegenlied)

By Johannes Brahms

Strum Pattern: 7
Pick Pattern: 7

Tenderly

Gu - ten a - bend, gut' Nacht, mit Ro - sen be - dacht, mit

Näg' - lein be - steckt, schlupf ' un - ter die Deck': Mor - gen

früh, wenn Gott will, wirst du wie - der ge - weckt, mor - gen

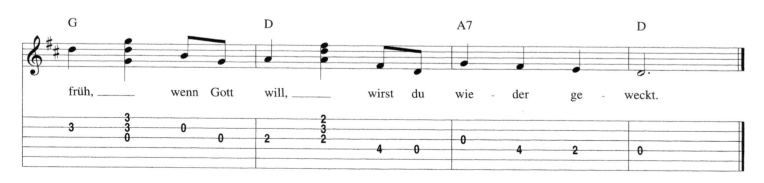

früh, wenn Gott will, wirst du wie - der ge - weckt.

Minuet

Music by Luigi Boccherini

Strum Pattern: 8
Pick Pattern: 8

Minuet in G
(from the Anna Magdalena Notebook)

Music by Johann Sebastian Bach

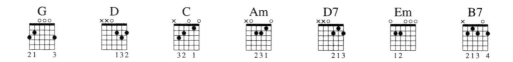

Strum Pattern: 8
Pick Pattern: 8

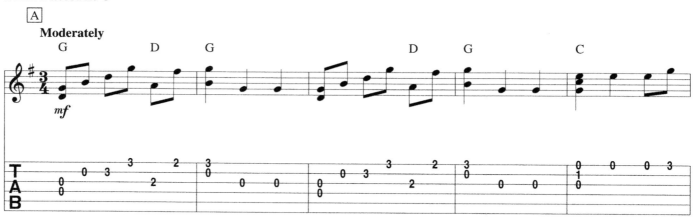

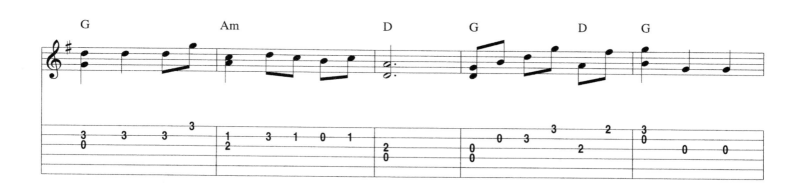

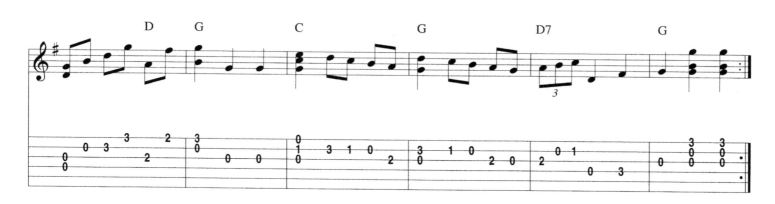

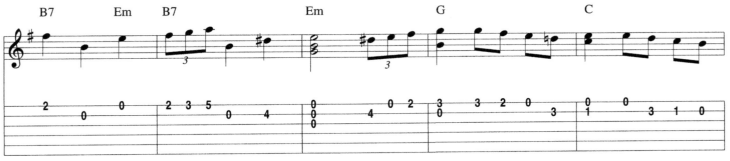

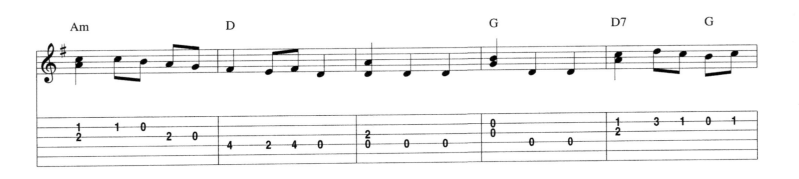

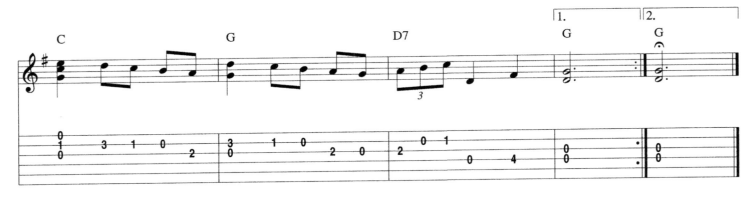

Minuet in G

(from the Anna Magdalena Notebook)

Music by Johann Sebastian Bach

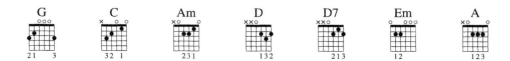

Strum Pattern: 9
Pick Pattern: 7

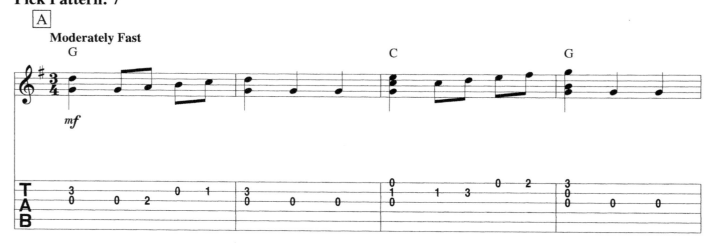

Minuet in G

Music by Ludwig Van Beethoven

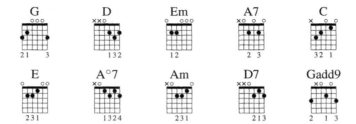

Strum Pattern: 8
Pick Pattern: 8

A

Moderately

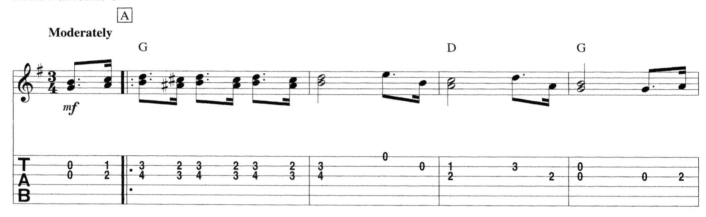

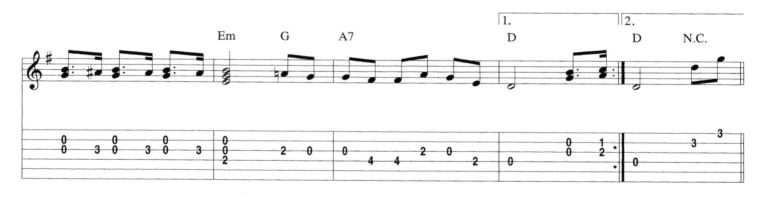

B

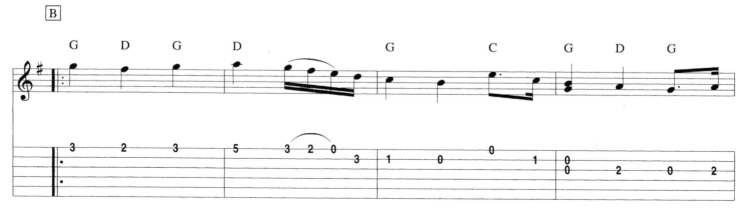

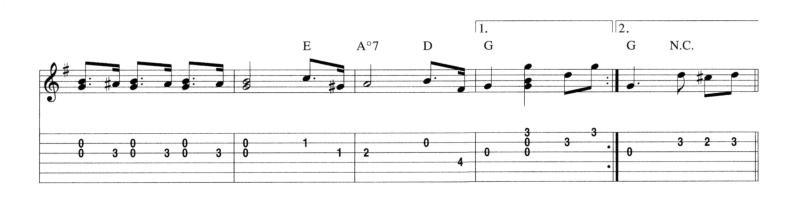

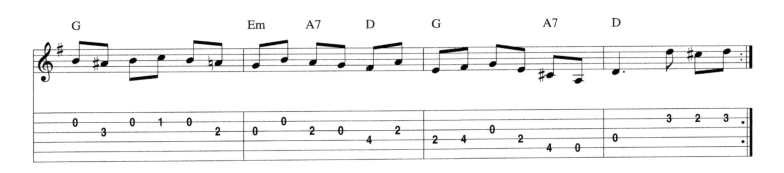

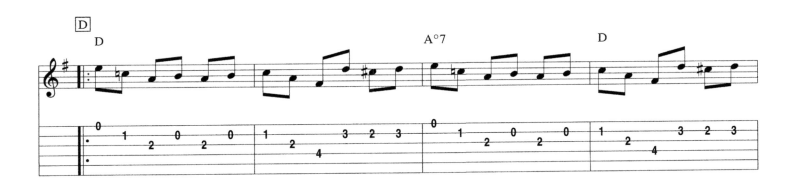

Morning
(from Peer Gynt Suite)

Music by Edvard Grieg

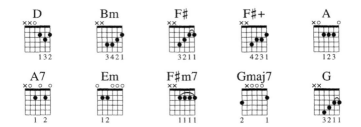

Strum Pattern: 8
Pick Pattern: 8

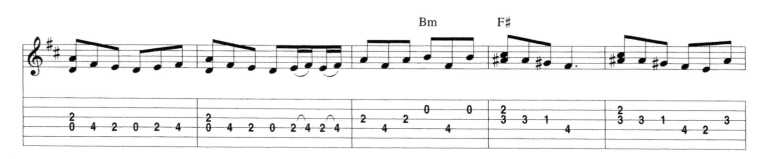

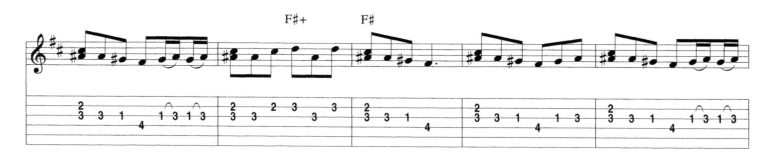

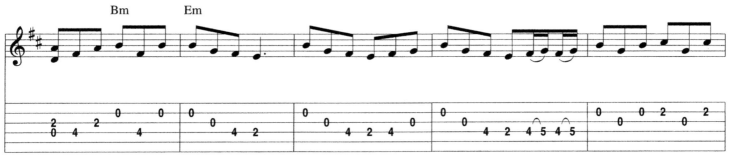

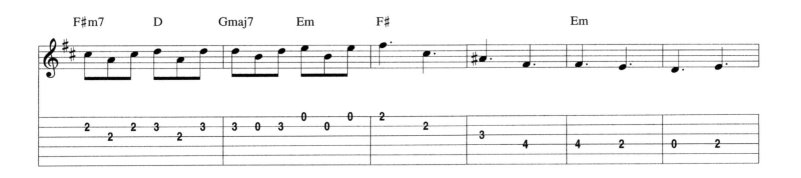

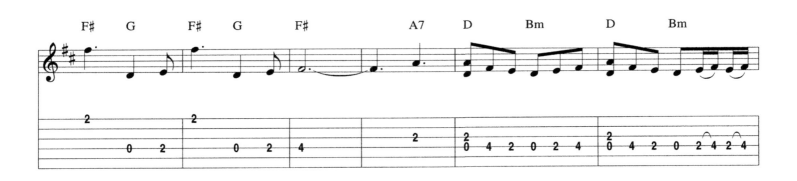

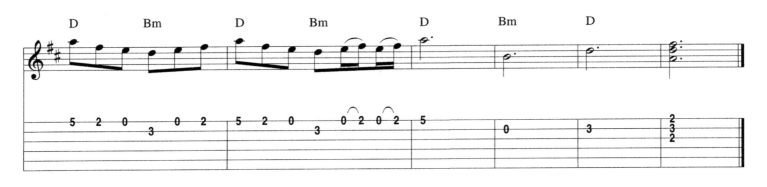

Ode to Joy
(Fourth Movement Theme, Symphony No. 9)
By Ludwig van Beethoven

Peter and the Wolf
(Ballet)

Music by Sergei Prokofiev

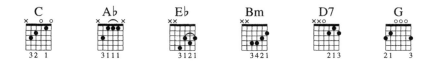

Strum Pattern: 5
Pick Pattern: 1

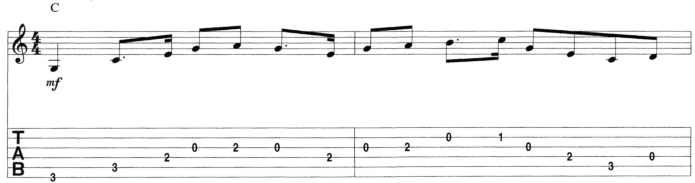

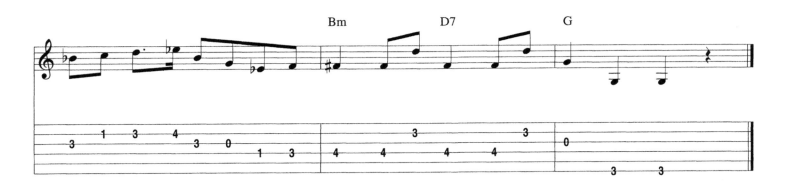

Pizzicato Polka

Music by Léo Delibes

Strum Pattern: 4
Pick Pattern: 3

Santa Lucia

Traditional

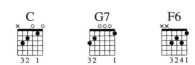

Strum Pattern: 8, 9
Pick Pattern: 8, 9

Verse
Slowly

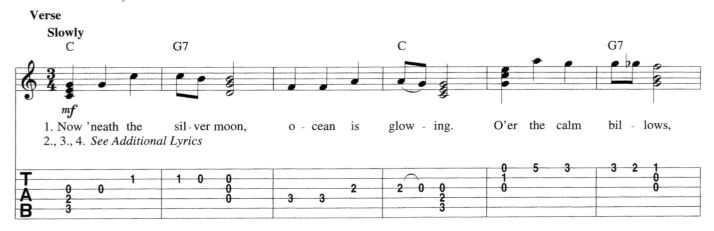

1. Now 'neath the sil - ver moon, o - cean is glow - ing. O'er the calm bil - lows,
2., 3., 4. *See Additional Lyrics*

Chorus

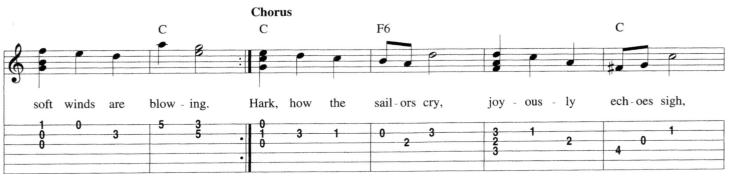

soft winds are blow - ing. Hark, how the sail - ors cry, joy - ous - ly ech - oes sigh,

To Coda ⊕   *D.C. al Coda* (take repeat)   ⊕ *Coda*

San - ta ___ Lu - ci - a, San - ta Lu - ci - a.   San - ta Lu - ci - a.

Additional Lyrics

2. Here balmy breezes blow, pure joys invite us.
   And as we gently row, all things delight us.

3. When o'er the waters, light winds are playing;
   Their spell can soothe us, all care allaying.

4. Thee, sweet Napoli, what charms are given.
   Where smiles creation, toil blessed heaven.

Sheep May Safely Graze

Music by Johann Sebastian Bach

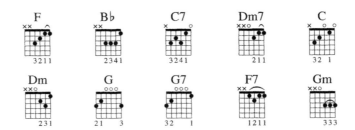

Strum Pattern: 3
Pick Pattern: 3

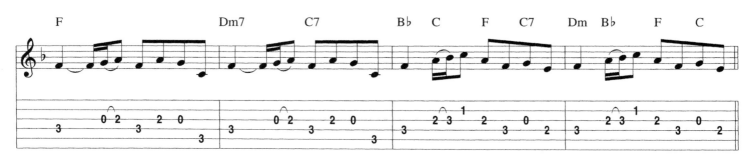

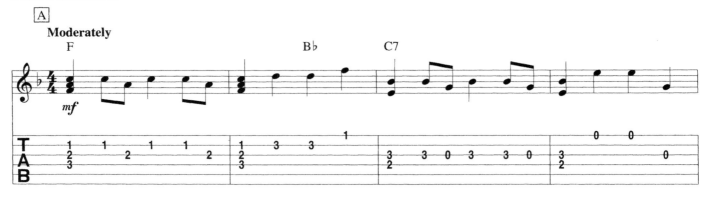

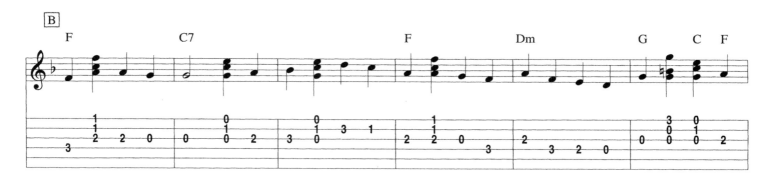

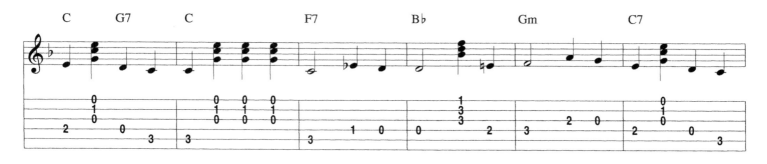

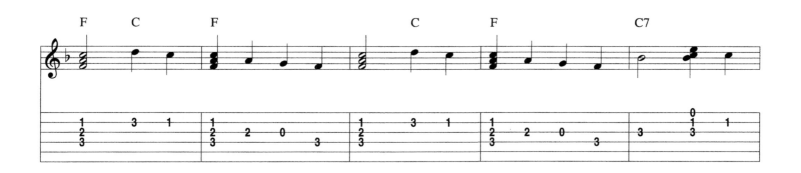

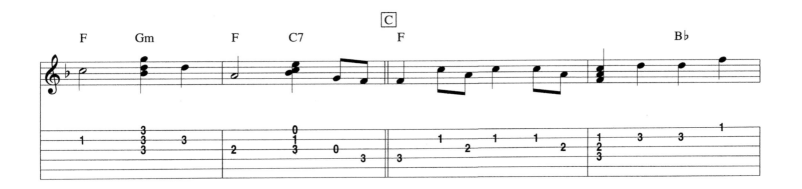

Surprise Symphony
(2nd Movement Theme)

Music by Franz Joseph Haydn

Strum Pattern: 10
Pick Pattern: 10

Toyland
(from Babes in Toyland)
Music by Victor Herbert

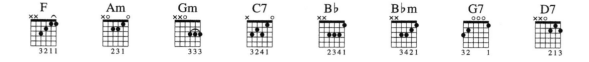

Strum Pattern: 8
Pick Pattern: 8

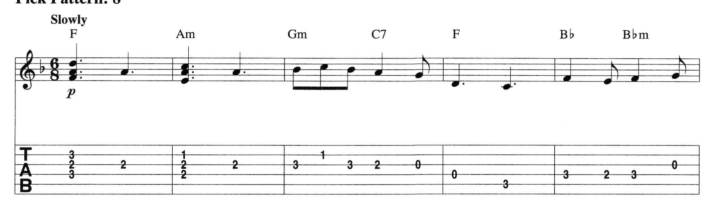

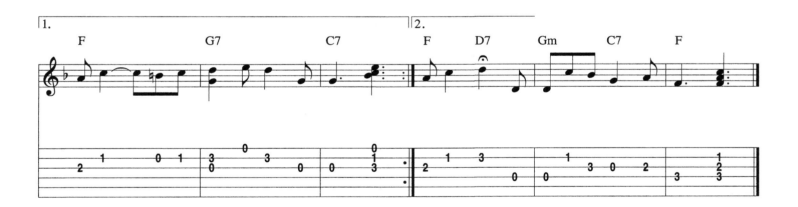

Volta

Music by Michael Praetorius

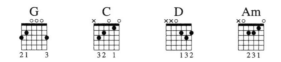

Strum Pattern: 7
Pick Pattern: 7

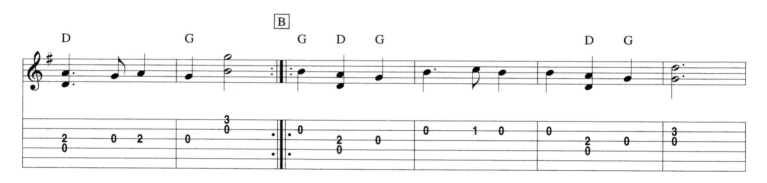

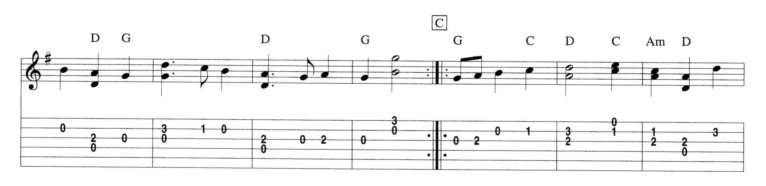